THE FLUTE PLAYER'S COMPANION

Volume 2
(Intermediate-Advanced)

Compiled and edited by
Edward Blakeman

Illustrations from the collection of
Tony Bingham

CHESTER MUSIC

For Toni and Sarah

INTRODUCTION

The contents of this companion have been chosen to assist the flute player's technical progress during the early years of study.

Flute technique, at whatever level, consists of five main points:

POSTURE
BREATHING
EMBOUCHURE
FINGERING
TONGUING

Posture is the basic poise and support of flute playing.
Breathing and Embouchure create and direct the sound.
Fingering translates the sound into music.
Tonguing adds final shape and articulation.

The ideal of good technical practice should be to master these points so that they can work effectively both **independently** and **interdependently**.

The studies in each of these two volumes have been arranged to complement work on the *Five Points of Technique*. The **Warming Up** exercises enable the player to attend to correct posture and general technical readiness for further practice. The **Tone** studies help to develop control of breathing and embouchure. The **Facility** studies encourage dexterity of fingering, and the **Articulation** studies exercise the tongue in a variety of ways.

The studies have been edited as regards phrasing and dynamics. Breathing marks, however, have been left to the individual player to add as a necessary part of exploring the musical structure of each study, and a successful study should sound like a piece of music! A few duets have also been included for ensemble practice. Brief biographical details of each composer, and the sources of the studies, are given on the Contents pages. The illustrations have been generously provided from the collection of Tony Bingham.

Any worthy companion should be interesting as well as instructive. Such, at least, is the aim of this collection.

Edward Blakeman

THE FLUTE PLAYER'S COMPANION
CONTENTS FOR VOLUME 2

GARIBOLDI, Guiseppe (1833-1905)   *20 Lyrical Studies, Op. 88*   **7**

Italian flautist. Soloist in Paris for most of his career. Composer of operettas and songs in addition to much flute music. Author of a flute method (c.1880).

KARG-ELERT, Siegfried (1879-1933)   *30 Caprices, Op. 107*   **5**

German pianist, organist and composer of various works featuring the flute.

KÖHLER, Ernesto (1849-1907)   *25 Romantic Studies, Op. 66*   **6 30**

Austrian flautist, though born in Italy. Solo flute of the Imperial Opera, Saint Petersburg for much of his career. Prolific composer of flute music, several ballets and an opera. Author of a flute method (c.1885).

KUMMER, Kaspar (1795-1870)   *32 Studies, Op. 129*   **10 29**

Saxon flautist. Musician at the court of the Duke of Coburg for most of his career. Prolific composer for the flute, and author of a flute method (c.1850).

MAHAUT, Antoine (?-c.1765)   *Flute Method* (1759)   **26***

Dutch flautist. Prolific composer of flute music, symphonies and songs. Died in Paris after fleeing there to escape his creditors.

PAGANINI, Nicolo (1782-1840) (arr. Jules Herman) (1830-?)   *24 Caprices, Op. 1*   **32***

Paganini: Italian virtuoso violinist and composer. Jules Herman: French flautist. Professor at the Lille Conservatoire from 1854-1902.

PRILL, Emil (1867-1940)   *24 Technical Studies, Op. 12*   **8 20**

German flautist. First flute of the Berlin Royal Opera, and Professor at the Berlin Hochschule from 1903 to 1934. Author of a flute method (1912).

QUANTZ, Johann Joachim (1697-1773) and **KING FREDERICK THE GREAT** (1712-1786)   *Flute Book*   **16 17**

Quantz: German flautist and flute maker. Court composer and flute teacher to King Frederick the Great of Prussia (an accomplished player and composer) from 1741 until his death. Author of the important book *On Playing the Flute* (1752).

SOUSSMANN, Heinrich (1796-1848)   *24 Daily Exercises, Op. 53*   **4 18**

German flautist and violinist. First flute at the Imperial Opera, Saint Petersburg from 1836. Prolific composer of flute music and author of a flute method (1839).

TAFFANEL, Paul (1844-1908)   *Sicilienne-Étude*   **11***

French flautist. Professor at the Paris Conservatoire from 1893 to 1908. The most influential player of his generation. Founder of the modern French School of flute playing, and author of a flute method (1923, with Philippe Gaubert).

TULOU, Jean-Louis (1786-1865)   *Duets* from *Flute Method* (1735)   **13* 25* 35***

French flautist. Professor at the Paris Conservatoire from 1829 to 1859. Virtuoso soloist, famous throughout Europe, and fierce opponent of the Boehm flute. Prolific composer of all types of flute music.

* denotes a study that has been abbreviated for this collection.

I
WARMING UP

'I always advise my pupils to practise scales in front of a mirror. Then they can watch their finger movements and whole manner of holding the flute. They can also detect many bad habits like distorted facial features and unnecessary movements of the head, arms and body.'

(*Boehm*)

As technique advances, it becomes even more important to maintain correct support and balance, both of the flute and the flautist. Flute playing may be tiring at times, but it should never be stressful!

Only the first part of each exercise is given for Nos. 1 and 2; the remainder should follow in sequence through the complete cycle of major and minor keys. Work them out and play them from memory in front of a mirror, so that you can observe every aspect of your technique.

2

Dorus

1.

Continue through all keys: major followed by relative minor.
Practise tongued and slurred, varying the tempo and dynamics.

Dorus

2.

Continue through all keys, modulating each time to the subdominant and changing registers where necessary.
Practise with the following articulations, and vary the tempo and dynamics.

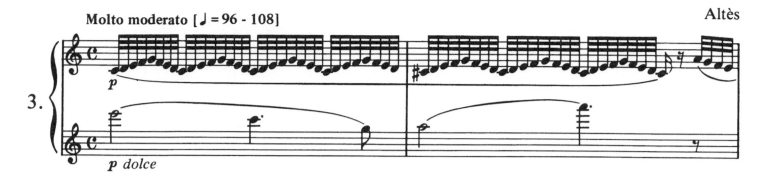

Molto moderato [♩ = 96 - 108]

Altès

3.

p

p dolce

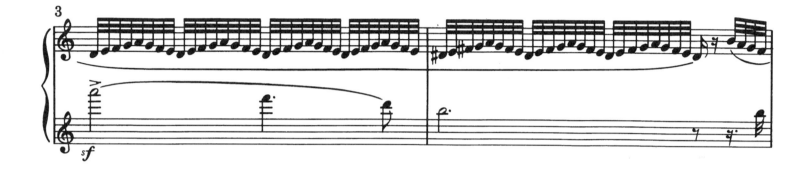

sf

sf

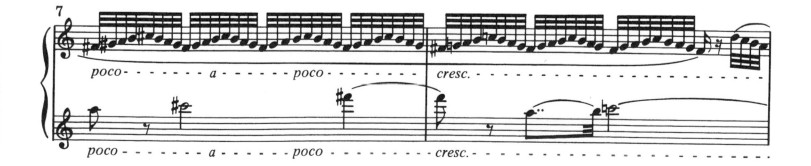

poco - - - - - - a - - - poco - - - - - - - cresc. - - - - - - -

poco - - - - - - a - - - poco - - - - - cresc. - - - - -

Altès

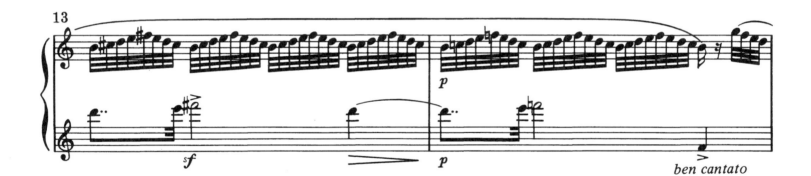

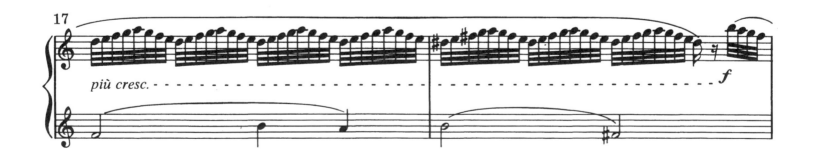

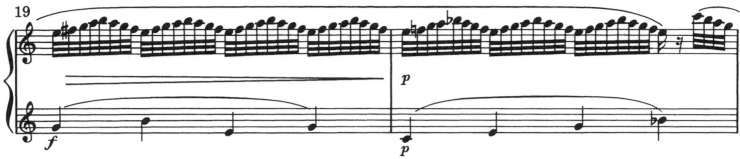

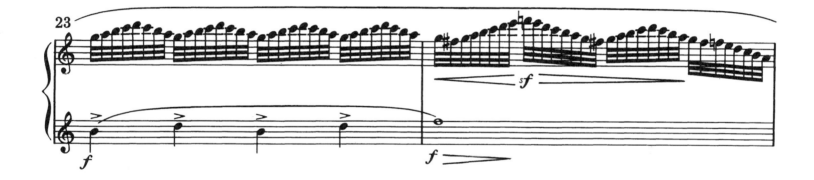

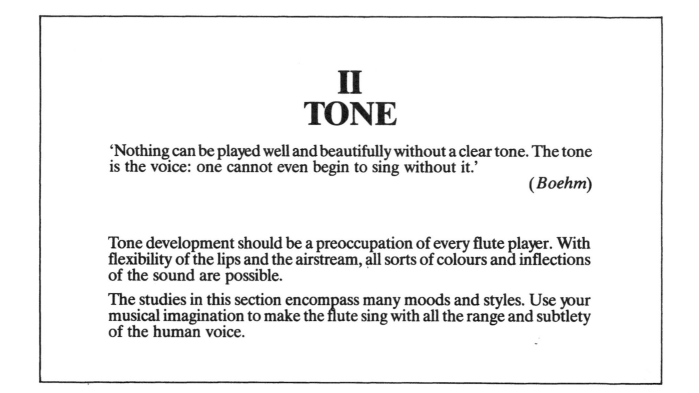

II
TONE

'Nothing can be played well and beautifully without a clear tone. The tone is the voice: one cannot even begin to sing without it.'

(*Boehm*)

Tone development should be a preoccupation of every flute player. With flexibility of the lips and the airstream, all sorts of colours and inflections of the sound are possible.

The studies in this section encompass many moods and styles. Use your musical imagination to make the flute sing with all the range and subtlety of the human voice.

Leggerissimo e grazioso

Karg-Elert

CANTABILE ALLA MODERNA

Köhler

Allegro maestoso

6.

f con ardore

Andantino con grazia

Gariboldi

7.

Prill

Largo ma non troppo

8.

p espress.

5

7

mf

9

12

mf

14

p

18

21

p

25

27

30

dim. - - - - - - - - - - - - - - - - - - - *pp*

THE SONG OF THE WIND

J. Donjon

Allegretto *(soutenez bien les notes du chant.)*

10. Largo ma non troppo

SICILIENNE-ETUDE

Tulou

Moderato

13.

III
FACILITY

'Those who take the trouble to practise patiently the complicated fingerings of every phrase until they are smooth and clear, make the fastest progress.'

(*Boehm*)

For fingering to be really efficient, intricate co-ordination patterns must be made as naturally as the movement of only one or two fingers. Otherwise fingering will hinder musical expression.

The studies in this section explore aspects of fingering in all registers, through a variety of keys. Aim at ease and economy of movement at all times.

Berbiguier

Allegro

14.

3

6

9

12

15

18

21

24

27

Drouet

15.

Quantz

16.

Quantz

17.

Soussmann

IRISH WALTZ

Camus

Prill

Allegro

20.

4

7

10

13

16

19

22

25

Vivace *[in the style of a Cadenza]*

Delusse

21.

Adagio　　　　　　　　　　　　　　　　　　**Allegro**

* The dotted bar lines at the end of each section are editorial.

Fürstenau

Boehm

23.

Finale

Andersen

Allegro con brio

24.

6

11

16

21

26

31

36

41

46

Allegro moderato

Tulou

25.

IV
ARTICULATION

'Articulation on an instrument is the equivalent of the correct enunciation or expression of the words of a song. It is important, therefore, to master the necessary art and practice of tonguing.'

(Boehm)

If the tongue is working freely, it can combine with the lips and the air-stream to shape and inflect the notes.

The studies in this section illustrate some of the complexities of articulation (including opportunities for double and triple tonguing). Aim at developing the lightness, precision and stamina of the tongue.

Mahaut

Allegro assai

26.

Allegretto leggermente

Demersseman

Kummer

Andersen

31. Allegro

D.C. al Fine

Quasi Presto

32.

7

VAR.I *

13

19

VAR. II

25

31

VAR. III

37

41

45

* in the original, these variations were I, VI and IX

Boehm

48

F. Donjon

34.

sempre staccato

Tremolo

sempre staccato

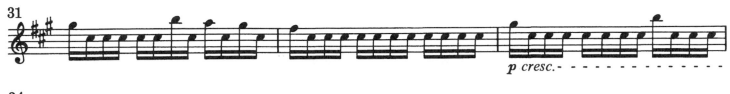

Tulou

35.

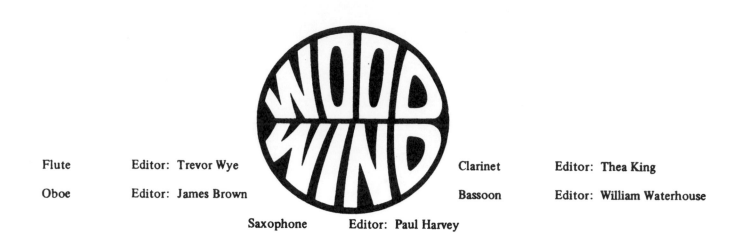

Flute	Editor: Trevor Wye		Clarinet	Editor: Thea King
Oboe	Editor: James Brown		Bassoon	Editor: William Waterhouse
	Saxophone	Editor: Paul Harvey		

A growing collection of volumes from Chester Music, containing a
wide range of pieces from different periods.

Also available:
CLARINET DUETS VOLUMES I, II & III
Further details on request

CHESTER MUSIC